John 14 - 17

30-DAY DEVOTIONAL

John 14 - 17

Simon Manchester
with Elizabeth McQuoid

FOOD
FOR THE
JOURNEY

INTER-VARSITY PRESS
36 Causton Street, London SW1P 4ST, England
Email: ivp@ivpbooks.com
Website: www.ivpbooks.com

First published 2017

British Library Cataloguing-in-Publication Data
A catalogue record for this book is available from the British Library.

ISBN: 978–1–78359–495–5
eBook ISBN: 978–1–78359–496–2

Typeset in Great Britain by CRB Associates, Potterhanworth, Lincolnshire
Printed and bound by CPI Group (UK) Ltd, Croydon, CR0 4YY

*Inter-Varsity Press publishes Christian books that are true to the Bible and that
communicate the gospel, develop discipleship and strengthen the church for its
mission in the world.*

*IVP originated within the Inter-Varsity Fellowship, now the Universities and Colleges
Christian Fellowship, a student movement connecting Christian Unions in universities
and colleges throughout Great Britain, and a member movement of the International
Fellowship of Evangelical Students. Website: www.uccf.org.uk. That historic association
is maintained, and all senior IVP staff and committee members subscribe to the UCCF
Basis of Faith.*

Preface

Can you guess how many sermons have been preached from the Keswick platform? Almost 6,500!

For over 140 years, the Keswick Convention in the English Lake District has welcomed gifted expositors from all over the world. The convention's archive is a treasure trove of sermons preached on every book of the Bible.

This series is an invitation to mine that treasure. It takes talks from the Bible Reading series given by well-loved Keswick speakers, past and present, and reformats them into daily devotionals. Where necessary, the language has been updated but, on the whole, it is the message you would have heard had you been listening in the tent on Skiddaw Street. Each day of the devotional ends with a newly written section designed to help you apply God's Word to your own life and situation.

Whether you are a convention regular or have never been to Keswick, this Food for the Journey series is a unique opportunity to study the Scriptures with a Bible teacher by your side. Each book is designed to fit in your jacket pocket or handbag so you can read it anywhere – over the breakfast table, on the commute into work or college, while you are waiting in your car, during your lunch break or in bed at night. Wherever life's journey takes you, time in God's Word is vital nourishment for your spiritual journey.

Our prayer is that these devotionals become your daily feast, a precious opportunity to meet with God through his Word. Read, meditate, apply and pray through the Scriptures given for each day, and allow God's truths to take root and transform your life.

If these devotionals whet your appetite for more, there is a 'For further study' section at the end of each book. You can also visit our website at www.keswickministries.org/resources to find the full range of books, study guides, CDs, DVDs and mp3s available. Why not order an audio recording of the Bible Reading series to accompany your daily devotional?

Let the word of Christ dwell in you richly.
(Colossians 3:16, ESV)

Introduction
John 14 – 17

Troubled. Confused. Uncertain.

After three years with Jesus, there was still so much the disciples didn't understand.

They were reeling from the news that someone in their inner circle would betray the Lord. Perhaps worse still was Jesus' prediction that their fiery and courageous friend Peter would deny him and that his death was imminent. It was unthinkable.

On this night of nights, with the agony of Calvary approaching and his own heart heavy, what would Jesus say to them? What comfort could he possibly offer? What essential truths did he want the disciples to grasp?

Reclining at the meal table, Jesus answered questions, taught and prayed for his disciples. In this final tutorial, he wanted to remind them of his love, his steadfast faithfulness and that he was utterly trustworthy. Regardless of what was to come, he was in complete control and the coming days would unfold according to his sovereign plan. He reassured them that his death would open up the way to heaven for them and, until he returned, his Holy Spirit would guide them into all truth. He anticipated the opposition they would face, but revealed how their union with him would keep them and make them fruitful. In these last moments together, Jesus was passionately interested in their holiness, unity and perseverance.

Today, disciples of Jesus still feel troubled, confused and uncertain. Perhaps we are asking different questions, but we still wrestle with doubts and concerns. Jesus longs to bring reassurance and, even now, he is praying for you. The apostle John invites you to listen in on this final tutorial and hear these essential truths. Let Jesus' words take root in your heart and mind, let them reshape the focus and priorities of your life and bring you comfort and hope.

Day 1

Read John 13:31 – 14:14
Key verses: John 13:31 – 14:3

....

Jesus said, 'Now the Son of Man is glorified and God is glorified in him. [32] If God is glorified in him, God will glorify the Son in himself, and will glorify him at once.

[33] 'My children, I will be with you only a little longer. You will look for me, and just as I told the Jews, so I tell you now: where I am going, you cannot come.

[34] 'A new command I give you: love one another. As I have loved you, so you must love one another. [35] By this everyone will know that you are my disciples, if you love one another.'

[36] Simon Peter asked him, 'Lord, where are you going?'

Jesus replied, 'Where I am going, you cannot follow now, but you will follow later.'

[37] Peter asked, 'Lord, why can't I follow you now? I will lay down my life for you.'

³⁸ Then Jesus answered, 'Will you really lay down your life for me? Very truly I tell you, before the cock crows, you will disown me three times!

¹⁴:¹ 'Do not let your hearts be troubled. You believe in God; believe also in me. ²My Father's house has many rooms; if that were not so, would I have told you that I am going there to prepare a place for you? ³And if I go and prepare a place for you, I will come back and take you to be with me that you also may be where I am.'

Worry is usually our default setting. We worry about our family, job, finances, singleness, reputation, the future and a host of other big and small issues. We've heard Jesus' command, 'Do not let your hearts be troubled', but we don't know how we could possibly apply it. Is Jesus really asking us not to worry?

His words in John 14:1 sound like the start of a conversation, but we're actually joining it part-way through. Jesus has just washed his disciples' feet, they have had their last meal together and Judas has left. Jesus has told them that he is going to die and rise again three days later, but they will not be coming with him on this particular journey; they are going to stay and love one another.

The only thing Peter hears from this whole conversation is that Jesus is going to die. And he objects! Jesus says he can follow him later, but Peter says, 'No, I'll follow you now; in fact I'll die for you. That's how capable I am.' Jesus immediately replies, 'Do not let your hearts be troubled. You believe in God; believe also in me.'

Do you see what Jesus is doing? He is saying, 'Peter, you are not that brave, you are not going to be that success-ful, you're going to disown me and you are not worth trusting in. Put your trust in something trustworthy, in someone who can deal with your fears. You trust in God; I am not inferior to God. Trust in me. I will take care of the future.' Notice how many times 'I' is repeated in verses 2–3. Jesus is saying, 'I go, I prepare, I'll come, I'll take – I, I, I. Trust me. I'll do this, not you, Peter.'

Jesus' answer to troubled hearts – then and now – is to trust him.

'Do not let your heart be troubled' – this is God's command to you today. The only real antidote to worry is trusting in Jesus. The problem is that many of us, like Peter, are DIY or do-it-yourself Christians. We like to depend on our own abilities. We want to do things ourselves and we can't quite accept that salvation is not something we have to contribute to. Maybe we need to say, 'It's going to be Jesus who will do the work: he will be the Saviour; he will carry me through. It's him I should be trusting, and there must be less focus on me and much more on him.' What do you need to trust Jesus with today?

Day 2

Read John 14:1–14
Key verses: John 14:2–3

....

> [2]*My Father's house has many rooms; if that were not so, would I have told you that I am going there to prepare a place for you? [3]And if I go and prepare a place for you, I will come back and take you to be with me that you also may be where I am.*

How can we be sure of heaven?

Jesus promises us a future with him: that's what will make heaven, heaven (verse 3). But how can we be certain?

In verse 2 Jesus says, 'I am going to prepare a place for you.' The NIV says, 'I am going *there* to prepare a place for you.' And so most people mistakenly think that Jesus is saying, 'I am going to heaven to prepare a place for you.' They imagine him going up to heaven with a hammer and chisel to prepare a room for us.

But Jesus is not saying that. He is saying, 'I am going *out* to prepare a place for you. I am not going *up* to prepare a place for you. I am going *out* – *out* of this room, *out* of this city, and when I am on the cross, I am going to be *out* of fellowship with the Father. And because I am going *out*, you can go *in*. Because I get the *exit,* you get the *entrance*; because I get *banished*, you get *welcomed*.'

Mark 15 describes the scene. On the cross Jesus cries out, 'My God, my God, why have you forsaken me?' And suddenly the temple curtain splits from top to bottom. Jesus was banished from his Father's presence so we could be welcomed in.

If getting to heaven depended on us, then we really would have something to worry about. But take heart, there is nothing we can do to earn our place in heaven; no tradition to keep or ritual we can perform. Your future is totally secure because it has nothing to do with your achievements, obedience or goodness. Your entrance into heaven, your place at the heavenly banquet, is certain solely because of Jesus' death on the cross. Because he paid the punishment for your sin, because he appeased God's wrath, your relationship with God is restored, your home in heaven secure.

Meditate on how much your place in heaven cost Jesus. Worship him today for the price he was willing to pay. Delight in the truth that you are greatly loved by an awesome God! 'For God so loved the world that he gave his one and only Son, that whoever believes in him shall not perish but have eternal life' (John 3:16).

Day 3

Read John 14:1–14

Key verses: John 14:4–7

....

⁴'*You know the way to the place where I am going.*'
⁵*Thomas said to him, 'Lord, we don't know where you are going, so how can we know the way?*'
⁶*Jesus answered, 'I am the way and the truth and the life. No one comes to the Father except through me.* ⁷*If you really know me, you will know my Father as well. From now on, you do know him and have seen him.*'

Sometimes we make Christianity sound too complicated. We talk in theological jargon, forgetting that, in essence, Christianity is all about a person – it is all about Christ.

Thomas has been following the conversation around the dinner table and in sheer desperation he blurts out, 'We don't know where you are going, so how can we know the way?' Jesus recognizes that explaining the crucifixion is too difficult for the disciples to understand. So instead, he says, 'I want you to focus on me, the person. Let's not talk so much about atonement, reconciliation, redemption. Let's just concentrate on me.'

And then he says the famous words in verse 6: 'I am the way and the truth and the life.' Thomas is asking, 'Is there any way to God?' And Jesus answers, 'I am the way.' This is the sixth time Jesus uses the phrase 'I am' in John's Gospel. 'I am' is a derivative of Yahweh, Jehovah, and therefore Jesus is using an explosive phrase when he describes himself again and again as 'I am'. He is declaring that he is the eternal God in the flesh. He also attaches a highly significant metaphor. So when he says, 'I am the bread' or 'I am the shepherd', there are huge Old Testament implications.

During this last supper together, Jesus wanted the disciples to know that they could trust him because he was the way to God: because he is the truth, he is reliable; and what flows from him is the life that is for ever, that is unbreakable. Jesus wanted these men to understand that knowing and trusting him is just the same as knowing and trusting God the Father.

Jesus is the way to God, the truth about God and the life of God, because he *is* God. Today Jesus says to you:

I am sufficient. I am sovereign. I am the God who sees you. I am your provider. I am faithful. I am righteous. I am gracious. I am compassionate and merciful. I am eternal. I am your refuge. I am your healer. I am your restorer. I am your defender. I am your rock. I am your redeemer.

Bring your circumstances and needs before him now, and imagine him responding by reminding you that he is 'I am . . .' Which of his character traits would he want to remind you of today?

Day 4

Read John 14:1–14
Key verse: John 14:6

....

6 Jesus answered, 'I am the way and the truth and the life. No one comes to the Father except through me.'

'Tolerance' is a popular word these days. In our multifaith, multicultural society, 'tolerance' is seen as the only way to preserve unity.

But what is tolerance? When people speak of tolerance, they often mean, 'I will love you as long as we can both agree that whatever we say is all true.' But making our love for people conditional on agreeing everything is true doesn't make sense – in the world or the church.

We must have a different understanding of the term 'tolerance', one that loves people regardless of disagreements on the issues. True tolerance says, 'I will love you whatever you say or do. I may completely disagree with what you are saying, but I will keep being patient and kind and I will stay with you.'

Although not primarily dealing with the question of whether there are many ways to God, this verse does stand in the face of plural religions. Jesus' statement, 'I am the way and the truth and the life. No one comes to the Father except through me', shatters the contemporary view of tolerance.

But Jesus can see more clearly, love more dearly and speak so plainly because he genuinely wants people to be safe and secure. If you are in a burning building and you happen to know that only one door is unlocked, there is nothing loving about saying to people in the building, 'Pick your door.' The loving thing is to push them, if necessary, towards the door that will open. This is what Jesus is doing here. He is lovingly saying that he's the door and we must come to him.

We need to be sensitive and wise in the way we share the gospel with our non-Christian family, friends and colleagues. Sometimes being silent is the best option! However, we can also get into a rut of not sharing our faith at all: essentially saying to those around us, 'Pick your door.' Ask God to help you push people through the right door – through your prayers, kindness, conversations, attitudes and actions. Pray for the opportunity to speak to one person about Jesus today. And when he gives you the opportunity, go for it!

Day 5

Read John 14:1–14
Key verses: John 14:8–11

....

> [8]*Philip said, 'Lord, show us the Father and that will be enough for us.'*
>
> [9]*Jesus answered: 'Don't you know me, Philip, even after I have been among you such a long time? Anyone who has seen me has seen the Father. How can you say, "Show us the Father"? [10]Don't you believe that I am in the Father, and that the Father is in me? The words I say to you I do not speak on my own authority. Rather, it is the Father, living in me, who is doing his work. [11]Believe me when I say that I am in the Father and the Father is in me; or at least believe on the evidence of the works themselves.'*

It would be so much easier if God wrote his will in the sky, spoke audibly or even appeared in a dream. If God spoke that clearly, we'd definitely obey him! Just a bit more information, just a little bit more clarity – surely that would make all the difference?

Philip thought the same. In verse 8 he says, 'Lord, show us the Father and that will be enough for us.' He has seen Jesus turn water into wine, heal the lame man, feed thousands, heal the blind and raise Lazarus from the dead. What Jesus has done and said is extraordinary, but still Philip is dissatisfied and says, 'I just wish I had a little more information.'

Jesus replies by telling Philip, 'If you have seen me, you have seen the Father.' And he goes on, 'The words I say to you I don't speak on my own authority. Rather, it is the Father in me, who is doing his work.' We expect him to say, 'The words I speak are the words the Father speaks.' But instead, he links the Word of God and the work of God. He is saying, 'My words are the Father's work. When I speak, God works. So believe that the Father and I are profoundly related and work together.'

Jesus' answer to Philip, and to us if we're dissatisfied, is to go back to his words and his works. Don't wait for God to speak across the sky: that's probably not going to happen. Say to God, 'If you work by your Word and I go back to your Word, would you do a new work in me? Would you renew my trust and my belief? Would you renew my repentance and my obedience? Would you renew my usefulness?'

Be encouraged: we have all the riches of Christ Jesus. We have the Scriptures, and the Holy Spirit is our teacher. We need simply to learn from this anguished conversation with Philip to go back to what we have and ask God to work with the Word that he has given us.

It is easy to look around at other Christians and become dissatisfied. They seem to be more spiritual than us, enjoying a deeper communion with God and receiving clearer guidance from him. Our knee-jerk reaction is to look for a quick fix, or search for the secret spiritual ingredient we must be missing.

Call the search off! The Bible assures us, 'His divine power has given us everything we need for a godly life through our knowledge of him who called us by his own glory and goodness' (2 Peter 1:3).

According to Peter and Jesus' words here in John, it seems that we determine how spiritual we want to be and we choose how close to God we want to be. Through the Bible and with the help of the Holy Spirit, we can get to know Jesus personally and intimately, and be equipped for holy living. What is holding you back?

Day 6

Read John 14:1–14

Key verses: John 14:12–14

. . . .

> *12 Very truly I tell you, whoever believes in me will do the works I have been doing, and they will do even greater things than these, because I am going to the Father. 13 And I will do whatever you ask in my name, so that the Father may be glorified in the Son. 14 You may ask me for anything in my name, and I will do it.*

Critics often claim, 'You can't take the Bible literally.' And these verses seem to add weight to their argument. Verse 12 certainly looks like an exaggeration, doesn't it?

If you have faith in Jesus, he says, you 'will do even greater things'. And if 'greater' means doing *better* things than Jesus, how can he be serious? Am I really going to turn water into wine? Am I really going to feed more people with a few loaves and fishes? Am I really going to bring more Lazaruses out of their graves? Impossible!

What Jesus means is that you are going to do things of greater quality. Those of you who put your trust in me, you are going to point people to me! You are not going to point people to a loaf of bread, but to the Bread of Life. You are not going to send people to a little lampstand, but to the Light of the World. You are not going to offer people resuscitation on a hospital bed, but the resurrection that outlasts the world. You are going to do greater things, things that all the miracles in John's Gospel were pointing to – you are going to point people to Jesus.

How will we do these things? By asking Jesus for help: 'And I will do whatever you ask in my name, so that the Father may be glorified.' But be careful not to assume that Jesus is giving carte blanche to our prayer requests. He is speaking here in the context of helping people come to him. He is promising that even though he is going back to the Father, he will help us point people to him. That's what he delights to do.

You have the opportunity of doing greater things than Jesus today! What an incredible thought and an awesome responsibility. Jesus knew that every day he had to be busy with his Father's work – and we must too. Whatever our daily lives look like, whatever our routines or responsibilities, our main role is to point people to Jesus. Think about all the people you will meet today. Will your actions, attitudes and words point them towards Jesus, or away from him? What opportunities could you take to point people to Jesus? Remember, he delights to help you. Will you ask for his help today?

Day 7

Read John 14:12–21
Key verses: John 14:14–15

....

> ¹⁴ *You may ask me for anything in my name, and I will do it.*
>
> ¹⁵ *If you love me, keep my commands.*

Have you been praying for years for the same friends or family members to become Christians? Are unanswered prayers making you feeling discouraged?

We looked at verse 14 briefly yesterday, but it's worth remembering that when you send up your prayers and ask God to act, you are not asking for some small-scale system to work. When we pray, it's not as if we are just calling a plumber and expecting him to come that day. It's not as though we are putting money into a machine and expecting to get a can of coke back in ten seconds. God may do amazingly speedy things, and we love it when he does so. But we also need to remember that when we pray to our Father, we are putting our requests to someone who is organizing an eternal, cosmic, majestic, huge plan. And if we ask how God is going to be glorified (verse 13), it may be that it is not going to be via a fast answer. It may be that God will be glorified through a long, brilliant process.

God hears every prayer that is uttered – not one of them gets lost. He hears our prayers better than a parent hears the cry of a child, but the whole process of his genius, all the machinery of heaven and the processes of eternity are being worked out by this great heavenly Father, so don't be too impatient.

I'm sure Jacob prayed for his son Joseph to return home that day (Genesis 37), but imagine if God had answered his prayers? What a tragedy! Instead, our great, loving, majestic God replied, 'You have absolutely no idea what I am going to do. I will bring him back, but it's going to be a long and most fruitful path. When he eventually does come back, astronomical things will have been done.'

So don't lose heart when you pray. Jesus says in verse 15, 'If you love me, keep my commands.' I wonder whether this is the command he means. I wonder if Jesus is saying, 'I am commanding you to keep praying because it's a great task I am leaving you to do in the world. I don't want you to forget to ask for help. Totally and brilliantly, I am presenting your case in heaven, and the Holy Spirit is going to help you and wonderfully supply all you need for your ministry in the world.'

Who are you praying for to become a Christian? If you don't pray regularly for a handful of people, start now! We were never meant to be active in pointing people to Jesus without covering all our efforts in prayer. We need the Holy Spirit's help – the task is impossible without him. And don't believe the lie that your prayers are just hitting the ceiling. Jesus is your advocate in heaven, bringing every one of your prayers before God's throne. As the Puritans used to say, 'The prayer of the believer is deathless.' If God seems delayed in answering your prayers, don't allow yourself to give up or become discouraged. Keep on praying and keep on trusting. Who knows what marvellous plan God is putting in place?

Day 8

Read John 14:15–21
Key verses: John 14:16–17

....

¹⁶And I will ask the Father, and he will give you another advocate to help you and be with you for ever – ¹⁷the Spirit of truth. The world cannot accept him, because it neither sees him nor knows him. But you know him, for he lives with you and will be in you.

How well do you know the Holy Spirit? He is probably the least understood member of the Trinity, and subsequently the subject of many debates.

The word 'advocate' appears five times in the New Testament – four times in these chapters of John's Gospel and once in the first letter of John. The Greek word *parakletos*, 'to be called alongside', has no real English equivalent. We will never find one word to do justice to the majestic, multiple ministry of the Holy Spirit. We know from Scripture that he teaches, convicts, leads, guides and helps; that he can be grieved, resisted and quenched;

and that he is a person, not a force or an 'it'. So the translators come up with words like Counsellor, Advocate, Paraclete, Helper, but none of them completely describes the great work of the Holy Spirit.

Wonderfully, verse 16 tells us that the Holy Spirit will be with us, 'for ever'. In the Old Testament the Holy Spirit left Saul (1 Samuel 16:14), and Psalm 51 records David's desperate plea that the Spirit wouldn't leave him. Here Jesus promises that the Holy Spirit will never leave us. He will move in and live with your sin until you see God face to face, and then you will be sinless. Aren't you grateful that the Holy Spirit stays with us for ever, that when we sin he doesn't leave us, and instead, he graciously convicts us?

Whereas the Holy Spirit 'lives with you and will be in you' (verse 17), the world doesn't know, and is hostile to, God's Spirit, for the secular person cannot appreciate the things of the Spirit. This doesn't make Christians any better or smarter than unbelievers; it only means that God's grace has brought us to Jesus and made us alive to the Holy Spirit's work. Interestingly, the word 'you' here is actually in the plural. The Holy Spirit will be in you individually and corporately. That's why when Christians gather together, we have such rich fellowship. That's why being part of the church family is so important.

Read the key verses again, noticing every time the word 'you' is mentioned. Do you see how personal and intimate the Holy Spirit wants to be with you? He is the ever-ready, ever-present 'God with us'.

No matter how much you grieve him, he will never leave you. But he longs for greater access to your heart, greater obedience, and to share greater ministry with you. He wants to work in and through you, to bring transformation and make you more like Christ. Why resist such an amazing gift? Today, invite the Holy Spirit to have his way in your life. Give him complete access to teach, guide, convict and help you.

Day 9

Read John 14:15–21
Key verses: John 14:18–20

. . . .

18 I will not leave you as orphans; I will come to you. 19 Before long, the world will not see me any more, but you will see me. Because I live, you also will live. 20 On that day you will realize that I am in my Father, and you are in me, and I am in you.

Sometimes we struggle to understand Jesus' words. Often, it is only in hindsight that their meaning becomes clear.

For example, what does Jesus mean when he says, 'I will not leave you . . . I will come to you'? Does he mean, 'I'm going to leave you on Friday and come back on Sunday'? Yes. Does he mean, 'I am about to leave you in forty days, fifty days, and I'll come as the Holy Spirit comes and takes residence in your life'? Yes. Does he mean, 'I am about to ascend, but one day I will return'? Yes – he means all of these things. But in verse 19 he says, 'You will see me', and so primarily he means that the disciples will see him quite quickly at the resurrection.

It is only after the resurrection and the coming of the Holy Spirit that the disciples finally understand Jesus' promise: 'Because I live, you also will live' (verse 19). This promise is also for us. He lives so that we who believe might live. As soon as you sent up your prayer to him for salvation, he committed himself to you, Shepherd to sheep: 'I will get you home. Because I live, you will live.'

I love the story of the nineteenth-century Baptist preacher Charles Haddon Spurgeon, who, when visiting his orphanage, got out a basin of water in front of the children and plunged his hands into it. He said to the boys and girls, 'Now, why don't my hands drown?' And one little boy said, 'Because your head's not in the water!' That's it, isn't it? Our head, the Lord Jesus, has risen. He is alive, always alive, so that we, his body, cannot die.

Critics discount it, our peers scoff at it, and even some theologians dismiss it. But Jesus' bodily resurrection is at the core of our faith. It is a doctrine we need to investigate, believe and articulate well. Today, stand on the truth of this marvellous promise: because Jesus lives, we too will live. The reality of Jesus' resurrection means that we will be with the Lord for ever. This is a promise for those who grieve for Christian loved ones, those who are anxious about the future, those who are suffering – it is a promise for all of us. Don't just think about Jesus' resurrection on Easter Sunday. Today, let his resurrection and your hope of eternal life govern your choices, the activities you get involved in, and what your mind dwells on.

Day 10

Read John 14:15–24
Key verses: John 14:21–24

••

²¹ *'Whoever has my commands and keeps them is the one who loves me. The one who loves me will be loved by my Father, and I too will love them and show myself to them.'*

²² *Then Judas (not Judas Iscariot) said, 'But, Lord, why do you intend to show yourself to us and not to the world?'*

²³ *Jesus replied, 'Anyone who loves me will obey my teaching. My Father will love them, and we will come to them and make our home with them.* ²⁴ *Anyone who does not love me will not obey my teaching. These words you hear are not my own; they belong to the Father who sent me.'*

Do you find it unsettling when Jesus says, 'If you love me, you will keep my commandments'?

Most of us would acknowledge that, even in our best moments, our love for Jesus is feeble and cool. Is Jesus actually saying here that obedience is crucial to our security? No, the faithfulness of Jesus is our security. He is faithful to us; his love for us makes us secure. So where does our love for him fit in? The Bible's answer is that our love for him increases the intimacy and enjoyment of that security.

Imagine taking your children on holiday. You help them into the car, put on their seat belts, shut the door and start driving. The security of your children is that you are driving, they are in their seats and the doors are closed. But those of you who have driven small children on long distances will know that their obedience is a big part of the happiness of the journey and a big part of the happiness of the holiday! I think that's what Jesus is saying here: our obedience has the wonderful effect of increasing intimacy, not security.

In verse 22, the other Judas questions why Jesus is going to show himself to so few people. Jesus refuses to discuss his strategy and replies, 'Don't question my plans, but question your heart, Judas. Is it open? Is it humble? We will make our home in such a heart.' This word 'home' in verse 23 is used only here and in John 14:2, where Jesus says, 'My Father's house has many rooms.' So Jesus is simply saying, 'If you are receptive and give a home to the living God, he will be receptive and give you an eternal home.' Welcome him, and he'll welcome you. Refuse him, and he'll refuse you.

Imagine Jesus as a guest in your heart. Are you making him welcome? Think about the books you read, the internet sites you browse, TV programmes you watch, relationships you have, clothes you buy and the language you use. Do they make Jesus feel 'at home'? The security of your relationship with God is not in doubt – that is dependent on Jesus' faithfulness. But your enjoyment of that relationship, your intimacy with God, is dependent on your obedience; it is dependent on how welcoming you are. Today, ask the Holy Spirit to show you what needs to change so that Jesus feels more 'at home' in your heart. Ask for his strength to make those changes.

Day 11

Read John 14:21–31
Key verses: John 14:25–27

....

> ²⁵ *All this I have spoken while still with you.* ²⁶ *But the Advocate, the Holy Spirit, whom the Father will send in my name, will teach you all things and will remind you of everything I have said to you.* ²⁷ *Peace I leave with you; my peace I give you. I do not give to you as the world gives. Do not let your hearts be troubled and do not be afraid.*

Do you enjoy looking through old photo albums? It's fun looking at ourselves – 'There I am!'; 'Look at my hair!'; 'What *was* I doing?' But not every photo in the family album is about us, and nor is every verse in the Bible. We need to beware of seeing ourselves in every verse.

Verse 25 is directed primarily at the apostles. The Holy Spirit is going to come, and in the next few weeks, months and years he will teach those apostles and remind them of everything Jesus said. This doesn't mean that the Holy

Spirit is going to teach them all the topics of the world, but he's going to teach them all they need in order to be people of faith and faithfulness. How does John remember the very long speeches of Jesus or what he said in chapters 5, 6 or 7? The Holy Spirit enables, teaches and reminds him. And Peter explains that the Holy Spirit drove the apostles on like little sailing boats, enabling them to record the Scriptures (2 Peter 1:21).

Of course, the Holy Spirit is going to teach every generation. But whereas the apostles were taught so that they could record the Scriptures, we are taught in order that we would appreciate the Scriptures. So please remember the things that you hear and are preached to you, and ask for the Holy Spirit's help to drive them home. Remember the words of Bible teacher John Stott who, before preaching, would pray the following prayer:

Heavenly Father, we bow in your presence.
May your Word be our rule, your Holy Spirit our teacher,
And your greater glory our supreme concern,
Through Jesus Christ our Lord.
(John R. W. Stott, *Between Two Worlds*, Eerdmans, 1982, p. 340)

And with God's Word in our hearts, it is no accident that peace follows (verse 27). Truth and peace always go together; they are related. Read what Jesus achieved on the cross, read the promises that apply to you, and know peace. Jesus does his atoning work on the cross and he gives his peace to us.

Today, know God's truth; enjoy his peace.

God comes into our frantic and fractured world offering us his peace, a peace that is so different from the fragile and fleeting cessation of conflict and chaos we aim for. God wants so much more for us. His deep-seated, unshakeable, never-ending peace can't help but spring from a restored relationship with him. Knowing that we are forgiven and loved by our holy heavenly Father, that we have a secure identity, an eternal purpose and a sure hope for the future, guarantees an 'out-of-this-world' peace.

If you feel out of touch with God's peace, then go back to his Word. Think back over the sermons you have heard recently and the Bible passages you have read in the last few days and weeks. What Bible truths have you been reminded of? Which of these truths do you need to cling on to today?

Day 12

Read John 14:21–31
Key verses: John 14:28–31

....

²⁸*You heard me say, 'I am going away and I am coming back to you.' If you loved me, you would be glad that I am going to the Father, for the Father is greater than I. ²⁹I have told you now before it happens, so that when it does happen you will believe. ³⁰I will not say much more to you, for the prince of this world is coming. He has no hold over me, ³¹but he comes so that the world may learn that I love the Father and do exactly what my Father has commanded me.*

Come now; let us leave.

Cults and other religions have had a field day with verse 28. Jesus' words, 'The Father is greater than I', at first glance seem to fly in the face of all we know about the Trinity, Jesus' divinity and his oneness with the Father (John 10:30). So what does Jesus mean here?

The clue is in the context. The Father is in heaven, Jesus is on the earth; the Father is in splendour, Jesus is in trouble; the Father is in perfection and Jesus is going to judgment. Where would you rather be? Jesus belongs in heaven. No wonder he is keen to return. He longs to return where he belongs, where the Father is, in a greater position and in a greater place.

Despite wanting to return to heaven, Jesus willingly goes to the cross. He knows the devil is coming to do what God has decided he will do (verse 30). Like a dog on a leash, Satan does not have free reign; his power is limited to what God permits. Nevertheless, Jesus goes to the cross because he loves you (John 3:16), but primarily because he loves the Father. His obedience and his love for the Father are all caught up in this absolutely perfect faithfulness to his Father (verse 31).

Love is not something we can contain; it always finds expression. Love for another person is demonstrated by a hug, a meal, help with the children, a cup of tea and a chat, and in a whole variety of other ways. Jesus' love for his Father is demonstrated on every page of the Gospels. Every act of obedience and every decision to be faithful was Jesus' declaration of love for his Father. How does your love for God find expression?

: What act of obedience or faithfulness is God asking of
: you today? Ask for the Holy Spirit's help and strength
: as you offer these acts as love gifts to God today.

Day 13

Read John 15:1–8

Key verses: John 15:1, 5

....

[1] I am the true vine, and my Father is the gardener . . .
[5] I am the vine; you are the branches. If you remain in me and I in you, you will bear much fruit; apart from me you can do nothing.

There is a saying: 'A picture paints a thousand words.' And here the image of the vine and the branches is an incredibly vivid description of the intimacy and fruitfulness God wants us to experience with him.

John 15:1 introduces it along with the seventh of the 'I am' statements in the book of John. But it is not a new image; the Old Testament is full of 'vine' teaching. 'You transplanted a vine from Egypt; you drove out the nations and planted it', but 'Your vine is cut down . . . Restore us, LORD God Almighty' (Psalm 80:8, 16, 19). Isaiah 5:2 says that the Lord had a vineyard and 'planted it with the choicest vines [Israel] . . . Then he looked for a crop of good grapes, but it yielded only bad fruit.'

When the Old Testament disciples failed to produce fruit, Jesus doesn't say, 'You New Testament disciples will produce good fruit.' He says, 'I am the vine; you are the branches' (verse 5). He'll produce the fruit through us. The Old Testament believers failed and we New Testament believers will fail, but he will not fail. He will bear the fruit that he is looking for.

Jesus is the vine, the Father is the gardener, believers are the branches and the purpose is fruit. But what is the fruit? It is not defined in this chapter, but it is referred to. For example, verse 8 says, 'This is my Father's glory, that you bear much fruit.' And verse 16 gives another clue – it's what God desires: 'I . . . appointed you so that you might go and bear fruit – fruit that will last.' So we can be pretty sure that the fruit is something that brings God glory. It is what he desires, that is, fellowship with Christ, loving one another and, if possible, being used by God to help other people come to Christ.

We all want to be fruitful – even unbelievers long to achieve something significant and consequential with their lives. But according to Jesus, true fruitfulness, fruit that will last, comes only from being a branch on his vine. So stop seeking significance and value from earthly achievements. Don't let a full inbox or recognition from colleagues, tutors and friends cloud your judgment. Instead, meditate on that image of the vine and the branches. You have been grafted 'into Christ'. Draw your life from him, allowing him to sustain you, and ask him to produce in you the type of fruit that will make a difference for eternity and bring him glory.

Day 14

Read John 15:1–8
Key verses: John 15:2, 6

....

²He cuts off every branch in me that bears no fruit, while every branch that does bear fruit he prunes so that it will be even more fruitful . . .
⁶If you do not remain in me, you are like a branch that is thrown away and withers; such branches are picked up, thrown into the fire and burned.

Have you ever tried the carrot-and-stick strategy? Perhaps you have used it to encourage good behaviour in your children, to motivate employees at work or to spur you on with your diet! A combination of rewards and punishments can be very effective.

Because we are complicated people and this 'remaining' is important, the Lord gives us a good mix of promises and warnings in verses 1–8. The promise is that Jesus desires to bear much fruit through you. The warning is that the fruitless branch goes to the fire. We need both the promises and the warnings in our Christian life – our fears need the promises; our sins need the warnings.

We may like to reduce Christianity to a slogan, but God is too wise for that. We need verses like John 10:28: 'No one will snatch them out of my hand.' And verses like John 15:2: 'He cuts off every branch in me that bears no fruit.' They don't contradict each other. We need them both. God is the perfect Pastor and he knows we are capable of lurching from fear to foolishness. He gives us warnings and promises so that we'll be safe.

If you find yourself in despair, go to John 10:28. But if you are in a casual position where nothing really matters and you don't care, and you think you are getting the best of sin and salvation, it might not be a bad idea to go to John 15:2 and ask yourself whether this is a fruitful time. As long as you don't let verse 2 preoccupy you, it is a good warning.

Even when we find ourselves being pruned – which by definition is hurtful, painful and costly – remember that the person doing this is the Father who loves you. None of it is done with sadistic carelessness, but rather with great affection, love and purpose.

Use the vine illustration to describe the current state of your spiritual life:

- Are you a dead branch, no longer connected to the vine or producing fruit, and needing to be chopped off?
- Are you a branch, grafted on to the main vine and producing fruit, regardless of external conditions?
- Are you being pruned by the gardener so that healthy growth and fruitfulness continue?

Which of God's warnings or promises do you need to take to heart today? Take seriously his warnings so that you don't become a dead branch. Cling on to his promises that every bit of painful pruning – in whatever form it comes – is for your good and for his glory. Remember, pruning is the only way a branch keeps on being fruitful. So don't despise the suffering or the discipline, but recognize it for what it is – the loving gardener shaping you into the image of his Son.

Day 15

Read John 15:1–8
Key verses: John 15:4, 7

. . . .

> [4] *Remain in me, as I also remain in you. No branch can bear fruit by itself; it must remain in the vine. Neither can you bear fruit unless you remain in me . . .*
>
> [7] *If you remain in me and my words remain in you, ask whatever you wish, and it will be done for you.*

How many sermons have you heard that finish with the challenge to 'keep reading your Bible and praying'?

It's a well-worn theme! Shouldn't we have moved on from the basics? Surely there is a danger that our faith will become cold, stale and formulaic because we have heard everything, read everything and sung everything?

Jesus is not interested in this kind of distant, professional relationship with you. He is too jealous a husband for that. He is not satisfied with a cold marriage. Instead, he longs for close, warm, intimate fellowship. The cross has removed the barriers in order to make that possible, and the Holy Spirit has brought new life into your heart to make that something you should long for.

The whole emphasis in verses 1–8 is to 'remain in Christ'. In fact, the Greek word that we translate 'remain' occurs ten times in the first eleven verses of this chapter. God's grace has grafted us into him, but we have a responsibility to stick close, to remain, to abide. That is surely why he says in verse 7, 'If you remain in me and my words remain in you, ask whatever you wish, and it will be done for you.' Do you see the combination of Scripture and prayer?

Jesus, the greatest teacher of all time, recognized that reading Scripture and praying provide the key to true fellowship. And every real Christian knows the difference between the dry orthodoxy that just turns the wheels, plays the game and goes to Keswick, and the fresh fellowship that Jesus seeks and gives. We need to ask him for it, we need to read the Bible for it and we need to pray for it. There is no shortcut to good fellowship with Jesus: the only way is by prayer and listening to his Word.

Be honest with yourself. Is your Christian life stale? Are you just going through the motions, or are you enjoying warm, deep fellowship with Jesus? Even if you feel close to him, there is always more intimate fellowship to enjoy. We can't exhaust God!

Jesus' death on the cross has removed the barrier; we can now draw close to him. But how close we get depends on us. The value we place on our fellowship with Jesus is measured by the effort we put into 'remaining in him'. There is no substitute for getting back to the basics – to reading your Bible and praying. What are you doing to 'remain in him'? How intentional are you being?

If you don't already have a prayer partner, arrange to meet up regularly with a Christian friend to pray together and discuss what God has been teaching you through the Bible. Encourage each other to keep pressing on in the faith and into deeper fellowship with God.

Day 16

Read John 15:9–17
Key verses: John 15:9–12

....

9As the Father has loved me, so have I loved you. Now remain in my love. 10If you keep my commands, you will remain in my love, just as I have kept my Father's commands and remain in his love. 11I have told you this so that my joy may be in you and that your joy may be complete. 12My command is this: love each other as I have loved you.

Many songwriters have told us, 'Love makes the world go round.' The world is certainly in need of true love, and in these verses Jesus teaches us about it.

Before we can love others, we need to know, first, where we ourselves stand. Although we don't deserve it, Jesus says, 'As the Father has loved me, so have I loved you.' In other words, 'Yes, the Father loved me perfectly and eternally, and I love you perfectly and eternally: that's a fact. You are a greatly loved person.'

Notice that Jesus uses the word 'loved' rather than 'loves'. He doesn't mean, 'I loved you in the past and I don't love you in the present.' He means, 'I loved you in the past and that's how I love you in the present. It's steadfast, fixed, a flag in the ground: I've loved you – it's established, it's decided.'

Second, recognize that obedience blesses the relationship (John 15:10). Jesus is not saying that your security hangs on your obedience; he is saying that your intimacy with him will be affected by your obedience. This means that you can speak to someone today about Jesus because your security does not depend on his or her response. You are loved at the start of the conversation and at the end, regardless of what takes place.

Third, realize what love means. Don't love people as you feel they should be loved or as the world loves; love them as you have been loved (verse 12). We are not going to lay down our lives and die for people and we are certainly not going to save them, but we can put away self-interest and give freely of ourselves for their good.

Imagine the difference it would make to our church and community if we loved people like this.

You are loved. We don't often spend time thinking about how much God loves us. It seems self-indulgent some-how. But allow yourself to dwell on this truth for a while:

> 'We are more than conquerors through him who *loved* us' (Romans 8:37).

> 'I no longer live, but Christ lives in me. The life I now live . . . I live by faith in the Son of God, who *loved* me' (Galatians 2:20).

> 'This is love: not that we loved God, but that he *loved* us' (1 John 4:10).

You are loved with a Calvary love. In the past, Jesus demonstrated his love for you on the cross, and that is how he loves you now. Never doubt that God loves you – passionately, completely and eternally. And there is nothing you can do to change that fact. 'Grace means there is nothing I can do to make God love me any-more and nothing I can do to make God love me any less' (Philip Yancey, *What's So Amazing about Grace*, Zondervan, 1997, p. 71).

Today, look for an opportunity to show that Calvary love to someone else.

Day 17

Read John 15:15–25

Key verses: John 15:18–25

∙∙∙

[18] If the world hates you, keep in mind that it hated me first. [19] If you belonged to the world, it would love you as its own. As it is, you do not belong to the world, but I have chosen you out of the world. That is why the world hates you. [20] Remember what I told you: 'A servant is not greater than his master.' If they persecuted me, they will persecute you also. If they obeyed my teaching, they will obey yours also. [21] They will treat you this way because of my name, for they do not know the one who sent me. [22] If I had not come and spoken to them, they would not be guilty of sin; but now they have no excuse for their sin. [23] Whoever hates me hates my Father as well. [24] If I had not done among them the works no one else did, they would not be guilty of sin. As it is, they have seen, and yet they have hated both me and my Father. [25] But this is to fulfil what is written in their Law: 'They hated me without reason.'

John Piper says that we in the West are not in the fires of persecution, but in the freezer! We probably won't get burnt at the stake, but most of us will have felt cold hostility when we've tried to share the gospel.

But we shouldn't be surprised. '*If* the world hates you' (verse 18) basically means, '*When* the world hates you.' Jesus is not talking about geography, but the hostile world system that says we are the centre of the universe. If the church agrees that the world rotates around us, we'll be left alone – we are saying what the world wants to hear. But if you say that *Jesus* is the centre of the universe, then you will feel hostility.

Jesus wants us to be equipped to deal with this, so he reminds us that we are not the first to experience opposition. Jesus was the lightning rod for three years; the church is the lightning rod, but we are actually suffering for him. He is the one who is hated, so don't expect to feel at home. If you belonged to the world, it would love you as its own, but you've been chosen out of the world, so you are something of an alien. Jesus reminds us, 'Remember what I told you: "A servant is not greater than his master." If they persecuted me, they will persecute you also' (verse 20). Jesus lived his life perfectly and he was hated. And if you live your life in a godly way, you will be hated too.

Verse 21 says that the world is blind and ignorant. But individuals are still guilty, because Jesus has come and they have no excuse for their sin. Those lovely people who live near us, and who in some ways are nicer than we are but don't acknowledge Jesus, are heading for hell – they are blind, but they are responsible. Tragically, the world is doing what God said it would do all along; it is just fulfilling the script: 'This is to fulfil what is written in their Law: "They hated me without reason"' (verse 25). God is not taken by surprise, and neither should we be.

We often assume that if only people could see how nice and caring Christians are, they would be won over to the gospel. Of course, believers should be winsome, and our love and kindness for others should be attractive. But if we proclaim with our words and lives that Jesus is the centre of the universe, we will face opposition.

So if you share the gospel with someone or invite them to an Alpha/Christianity Explored course and they respond badly, don't think, 'I should have done that better; someone else could have done that more effectively.' Don't be discouraged by hatred or hostility. Instead, keep telling people about Jesus and keep putting him at the centre of your world and praying that blind eyes would be open to God's truth. Fix your eyes on Christ and leave the results with him.

Day 18

Read John 15:18–27
Key verses: John 15:26–27

....

26When the Advocate comes, whom I will send to you from the Father – the Spirit of truth who goes out from the Father – he will testify about me. 27And you also must testify, for you have been with me from the beginning.

Have you ever taken part in a race? Do you realize that you are actually part of a relay team right now?

Jesus says, 'The Holy Spirit who is in you for ever and will teach you is going to testify; that is his great delight. And you will testify because you've been with me from the beginning.' Now of course we haven't been with Jesus from the beginning like the apostles had, but we are going to testify as part of the relay team, and he will be with us.

The Holy Spirit is in charge of the case for Christ; he is testifying to the world about Jesus. He orchestrates it, supervises it; he is not surprised by any apparent setbacks and he knows exactly what he is doing. Imagine if it were up to the bishops or the mission organizations to put forward the case for Christ. Thankfully, the Holy Spirit is in charge of the testifying and, amazingly, he wants to use us.

This doesn't mean we have to get on a soapbox or preach a sermon. We are asked to 'be wise' (Colossians 4:5). Sometimes this will mean initiating a conversation about Christ (Colossians 1:28); at other times it will mean answering somebody's question (Colossians 4:6).

You are part of the Holy Spirit's relay team, and Jesus gives you this promise: 'And surely I am with you always, to the very end of the age' (Matthew 28:20).

Whether you are a first-generation Christian or you come from a family of believers, you have an amazing heritage. You are part of a long line of relay racers that stretches right back to the earliest pages of the Old Testament. Thank God for those men and women who passed the baton of faith to you. Ask God for help to run your section of the race faithfully and pass the baton on to others.

Today, be alert to the Holy Spirit's promptings to testify for Christ. Ask the Holy Spirit to give you the right words to say, and keep your eyes open for these God-given opportunities. Watch out – they may be simple openings such as someone at work, college or the centre where you volunteer, asking you, 'What did you do this weekend?' Be honest and say that you went to church and listened to a message from the Bible. See where the Holy Spirit takes your conversation!

Day 19

Read John 16:1–11
Key verses: John 16:5–7

....

> [5]*Now I am going to him who sent me. None of you asks me, 'Where are you going?' *[6]*Rather, you are filled with grief because I have said these things. *[7]*But very truly I tell you, it is for your good that I am going away. Unless I go away, the Advocate will not come to you; but if I go, I will send him to you.*

Did Jesus get it wrong?

In John 13:36, Peter asked, 'Lord, where are you going?' In John 14:5, Thomas said, 'Lord, we don't know where you are going.' So why did Jesus say in John 16:5, 'None of you asks me, "Where am I going?"'?

Jesus' point is that his disciples have been concerned that he is leaving, but not where he is going. Just as you might say to someone who walks out of church during the service, 'Where are you going?', you're not interested in where they are going; you're concerned that they are leaving.

These disciples have been with Jesus for three years, yet they are utterly self-preoccupied. They are not interested in him or his mission. What must it be like for Jesus to have a body of believers like us who are so self-excited and self-preoccupied? It's amazing that he puts up with us. Just imagine having to listen to everybody's prayers – 85 million requests for a parking spot every second!

And the disciples are so distracted that they miss the big issue Jesus wants to tell them about. In verse 7 he says, 'It's for your good that I am going away. Unless I go away, the Advocate will not come to you; but if I go, I will send him.' Jesus wanted the disciples and us to understand that he needed to die and rise again so that we can enjoy intimate fellowship with God, and the Spirit is the proof or seal of that intimacy. The Holy Spirit brings new life, helps us understand the Scriptures and pray, makes us fruitful and gives us access to God's presence.

Take care not to be so preoccupied with 'self' that you no longer hear God speak or see what really matters.

It is easy to be so caught up in the minutiae of daily life, praying about our own needs and concerns, that we forget to look to Christ. We forget about the big picture of salvation history and the eternal plans God has for us. Lift up your eyes: refocus on Christ, the truths of the gospel and what God wants to do in and through you.

> So if you're serious about living this new resurrection life with Christ, *act* like it. Pursue the things over which Christ presides. Don't shuffle along, eyes to the ground, absorbed with the things right in front of you. Look up, and be alert to what is going on around Christ – that's where the action is. See things from *his* perspective.
> (Colossians 3:1–2, MSG, emphasis added)

Use Colossians 3 to help you refocus on some of God's priorities for you.

Day 20

Read John 16:1–11
Key verses: John 16:8–11

....

> [8]*When he comes, he will prove the world to be in the wrong about sin and righteousness and judgment:* [9]*about sin, because people do not believe in me;* [10]*about righteousness, because I am going to the Father, where you can see me no longer;* [11]*and about judgment, because the prince of this world now stands condemned.*

How will the Holy Spirit 'prove the world to be in the wrong'?

Will there be a heavenly court case where the Spirit convinces God that people are guilty and God suddenly admits, 'Oh yes, you're right. They're sinful.'

Of course not! God already knows we are sinful. The Spirit's work is to drive this conviction home in *our* hearts. Jesus explains that the Holy Spirit will bring conviction of:

- *Sin*: 'because people do not believe in me' (verse 9). Not believing in Jesus is a good definition of sin. Sin is not just the random lies we told or random lust we felt, but that we were fundamentally wrong about Jesus. And so the Spirit clears the fog, and we suddenly say, 'It's all about him.'

- *Righteousness* (verse 10). As people hear the gospel, they will realize that the righteousness of Christ is massive and their righteousness is pitiful. No longer do we have a low view of Jesus and a high view of self; now we have a high view of Jesus and a low view of self. Everything has been turned the right way up.

- *Judgment* (verse 11). Partly this is recognizing the judging work of Jesus winning victoriously at the cross. But partly it is a healthy fear of judgment causing us to turn to Christ.

The Spirit shames unbelievers into seeing that their view of Jesus is hopeless, their view of righteousness is inadequate and their view of judgment is plain wrong. We might say that sin has been shown to be deeper than we ever realized, righteousness higher than we ever realized and judgment closer than we ever realized. And so we call to Christ, and everything about him becomes clear, everything about self becomes clear and we move out of the fog and into the light.

We prefer to dwell on the comforting work of the Holy Spirit: how he illuminates God's Word to us, reassures us that we are children of God and gives us peace. But today, thank God that the Holy Spirit convicts, for without his conviction no-one could be saved! Pray for your various church ministries where the gospel is shared. Pray that the Holy Spirit would be active in people's hearts, convicting them of sin, righteousness and judgment.

And remember, the Holy Spirit's work doesn't end when we are saved. Today, invite him to convict you of the sins you are still holding on to; to show you the areas where Christ has to become greater and you need to become less; and, in the light of imminent judgment, to give you his power to live a holy life.

Day 21

Read John 16:1–11
Key verses: John 16:8–11

....

> [8] *When he comes, he will prove the world to be in the wrong about sin and righteousness and judgment:* [9] *about sin, because people do not believe in me;* [10] *about righteousness, because I am going to the Father, where you can see me no longer;* [11] *and about judgment, because the prince of this world now stands condemned.*

It's easy to get discouraged.

As we look again at verses 8–11, we may wonder why the Holy Spirit doesn't seem to be doing much convicting. In the West, at least, the church is not growing.

But when the work of evangelism is hard, don't fall into the trap of thinking that things are too difficult for God. Don't imagine God sitting in heaven wringing his hands just wishing someone would take him seriously. That's a man-centred view. The Bible's view is that God is utterly sovereign.

Our role is to keep going with the task. We must respond to God ourselves and then tell others about him the best we can – that's our job. Remember Jesus doing miracles and preaching in the cities, and nobody is taking any notice of him, and he says, 'I thank you, heavenly Father, because you hide, you reveal, you are totally in charge' (see Matthew 11:25). Then he suddenly turns round and says, 'Come to me, all you who are weary and burdened, and I will give you rest' (verse 28), because the gospel can't be stopped. It goes on like a river; if it hits a rock, it moves round it. It climbs a fence like a vine; if it hits a post, it climbs over it.

Just keep moving with the gospel and don't give up. God knows what he is doing.

Do you have a man-centred or a Bible view of evangelism? Be encouraged that although we might not see much gospel fruit, God is sovereign and all over the world people are becoming Christians. Meditate on these Bible verses to remind yourself of the unstoppable power of the gospel. Today, pray for the parts of the world where Christianity is spreading fast. And pray that we would not give up, but keep sharing our faith and letting the gospel loose in our communities.

> As the rain and the snow
>   come down from heaven,
> and do not return to it
>   without watering the earth
> and making it bud and flourish,
>   so that it yields seed for the sower and
>   bread for the eater,
> so is my word that goes out from my mouth:
>   it will not return to me empty,
> but will accomplish what I desire
>   and achieve the purpose for which I sent it.
> (Isaiah 55:10–11)

For I am not ashamed of the gospel, because it is the power of God that brings salvation to everyone who believes.
(Romans 1:16)

> All people are like grass,
>   and all their glory is like the flowers of the field;
> the grass withers and the flowers fall,
>   but the word of the Lord endures for ever.
> (1 Peter 1:24–25)

Day 22

Read John 16:1–15
Key verses: John 16:12–15

....

12 I have much more to say to you, more than you can now bear. 13 But when he, the Spirit of truth, comes, he will guide you into all the truth. He will not speak on his own; he will speak only what he hears, and he will tell you what is yet to come. 14 He will glorify me because it is from me that he will receive what he will make known to you. 15 All that belongs to the Father is mine. That is why I said the Spirit will receive from me what he will make known to you.

Has anyone ever said to you, 'God has told me . . .' and launched into a viewpoint that is totally at odds with what the Bible teaches?

The problem with this is that the Holy Spirit is not an independent thinker who speaks and acts contrary to how God has spoken and acted in his Word.

As John points out, the Holy Spirit is like an executor of a will. He passes on truth; he doesn't invent or withhold information. His role is to pass on what he has been given. He guides us into all the truth we will need for salvation and service.

Here in John 16:13, Jesus is launching the New Testament from the upper room. He says, 'He [the Holy Spirit] will guide you into all the truth . . . and tell you what is yet to come.' And Peter corroborates this in his letter when he explains that the apostles were driven by the Holy Spirit to record the Holy Scriptures (2 Peter 1:21). And so the Holy Spirit leads us into the Word because that's where the riches and treasures are found, but also because he is obedient to his task. His whole aim is to glorify Jesus: his work throughout the Old Testament is to get ready for Jesus, and his work throughout the New Testament is looking to Jesus.

A comment by one of the bishops in Sydney struck me deeply. He said, 'I wonder whether the Holy Spirit is interested in what we are doing in proportion to our interest in the glory of Christ?'

How interested are you in the glory of Christ? It's difficult to unravel our motivations, but think through the ministries you are involved in, the voluntary work you do, your studies or employment, the role you have in your family, where you spend your free time and money. How different would it look to do each of these things for the glory of Christ?

> Not to us, LORD, not to us
> > but to your name be the glory,
> > because of your love and faithfulness.
>
> (Psalm 115:1)

Day 23

Read John 16:16–23
Key verses: John 16:19–22

∙∙

[19] Jesus saw that they wanted to ask him about this, so he said to them, 'Are you asking one another what I meant when I said, "In a little while you will see me no more, and then after a little while you will see me"? [20] Very truly I tell you, you will weep and mourn while the world rejoices. You will grieve, but your grief will turn to joy. [21] A woman giving birth to a child has pain because her time has come; but when her baby is born she forgets the anguish because of her joy that a child is born into the world. [22] So with you: now is your time of grief, but I will see you again and you will rejoice, and no one will take away your joy.'

Most of us have a list of questions we would like to ask Jesus when we meet him. I suspect that when we see him, we will be too busy worshipping him to ask the questions. But having questions is OK.

In verses 16–23, Jesus is keen to answer the question the disciples are grappling with: what does he mean when he says, 'In a little while you will see me no more, and then after a little while you will see me'? Does Jesus mean, 'I'm leaving at Calvary; I'm back at Easter'? Does he mean, 'I'm leaving at the Ascension; I'll be back at Pentecost by the Spirit'? Does he mean, 'I'm leaving at the Ascension and I'll be back at the Second Coming'? Well, all three of them involve grief and joy, don't they? All three of them would fit the gospel.

I think we can be pretty sure, however, that Jesus means he's leaving at Calvary and coming back at the resurrection. That's his primary meaning, because the weeping is appropriate to the weekend more than it is to the fifty days or the 2,000 years, and the childbirth illustration is a relatively short struggle, not one that will be drawn out over weeks or years.

Verse 22 is a treasure of a text, isn't it? 'Now is your time of grief, but I will see you again and you will rejoice, and no one will take away your joy.' That's what Jesus said to the apostles, and the principle is utterly true for us today, especially when we say farewell to someone we love. The Lord says to us, 'Now is your time of grief', but you will see them again, 'and you will rejoice, and no one will take away your joy'. The reunion of 1 Thessalonians 4 is just around the corner.

'Now is your time of grief.' Grief comes in many guises: the loss of a loved one; intense sadness at the end of a marriage; coming to terms with long-term suffering; seeing hopes and dreams for the future come crashing down; acknowledging that your special needs child will never experience the life you wished for them. Grief is intertwined with life now; joy and sorrow go hand in hand. But one day in heaven we will see Jesus. There will be no more tears; our joy will be unquenchable. Can you imagine it? Let the impact of verse 22 sink into your heart and give you hope today:

> Then I saw 'a new heaven and a new earth' . . . And I heard a loud voice from the throne saying, 'Look! God's dwelling-place is now among the people, and he will dwell with them. They will be his people, and God himself will be with them and be their God. He will wipe every tear from their eyes. There will be no more death or mourning or crying or pain, for the old order of things has passed away.'
>
> He who was seated on the throne said, 'I am making everything new!'
> (Revelation 21:1, 3–5)

Day 24

Read John 16:23–33
Key verses: John 16:23–28

....

²³ *In that day you will no longer ask me anything. Very truly I tell you, my Father will give you whatever you ask in my name.* ²⁴ *Until now you have not asked for anything in my name. Ask and you will receive, and your joy will be complete.*

²⁵ *Though I have been speaking figuratively, a time is coming when I will no longer use this kind of language but will tell you plainly about my Father.* ²⁶ *In that day you will ask in my name. I am not saying that I will ask the Father on your behalf.* ²⁷ *No, the Father himself loves you because you have loved me and have believed that I came from God.* ²⁸ *I came from the Father and entered the world; now I am leaving the world and going back to the Father.*

We get used to ending our prayers 'in Jesus' name', don't we? It trips off our tongues and means hardly anything to us.

For three years the disciples had been asking Jesus for things, but now their prayer life was going to be radically different because Jesus was going and the Spirit was coming. Their prayers, and ours, would now be 'in Jesus' name'.

For us it may just have become a formula, but God the Father never gets used to hearing 'in Jesus' name'. It never bores him or becomes predictable, and it never grows stale. When the Father hears 'in Jesus' name', everything gets moving. Just as if you were a waiter at some special function and the Prime Minister asked you for some butter. You go to the kitchen and you are a nobody, but when you say, 'The Prime Minister has asked for butter', everything gets moving, doesn't it?

When you say your prayers 'in Jesus' name', that's a loaded phrase. It may not mean much to you, but it means everything to the Father. He has made sure that it carries huge significance; all the strength and wisdom are found in him.

'In Jesus' name' is not a magic formula that ensures we receive everything we ask for; it is the only way we can approach God. Jesus' death opened the way to God for us (1 Timothy 2:5). When you pray today, know that God embraces you warmly, but you are standing on holy ground, and your access to the Almighty was costly. Prayer is a privilege to use often, but never to be taken casually.

'In Jesus' name' is how we approach God, but it also shapes the content of our prayers. It means praying according to Jesus' agenda, purpose and will, and praying for things that will honour and glorify him.

Think about your prayers – how you approach God and the words you say. If you are stuck in a rut or your prayers seem like a shopping list, try something new. For example, today, write out your prayers so you can be more intentional about what you're saying to God.

Day 25

Read John 17:1–26
Key verses: John 17:1–5

....

¹*After Jesus said this, he looked towards heaven and prayed:*

'Father, the hour has come. Glorify your Son, that your Son may glorify you. ²For you granted him authority over all people that he might give eternal life to all those you have given him. ³Now this is eternal life: that they know you, the only true God, and Jesus Christ, whom you have sent. ⁴I have brought you glory on earth by finishing the work you gave me to do. ⁵And now, Father, glorify me in your presence with the glory I had with you before the world began.'

After all the waiting, it is finally over.

'The hour has come': literally, the *time* has come.

This hour has been a long time coming. The wedding at Cana (John 2): the hour has not yet come; Jesus talking with his brothers (John 7): the hour has not yet come; the Greeks arrive (John 12): the hour has not yet come. And now in John 17 the hour has finally come! The hour of the cross, the glorification followed by the resurrection and ascension, the work that Jesus has come for, has finally come.

And so Jesus prays. You might ask, 'Why would Jesus pray? It's all organized. God is sovereign, so why pray?' It never occurs to Jesus not to pray. Jesus knows the Father is sovereign, as well as loving and wise, and therefore he is the best person to speak to, and so that's what he does.

Do we turn to prayer as readily?

Our prayer life will never be free from doubt, guilt, tiredness, struggle, preoccupation and all sorts of things. There is never going to be a book, DVD or conference that will make praying easy. Prayer is part of the spiritual battle (Ephesians 6). Speaking to the invisible God, although we have access, although we are intimate, although the Holy Spirit helps us, is nevertheless difficult.

But keep praying! Prayer is crucial: it is fellowship with God, it puts joy and hope into our Christian walk and it is God's gift to us.

When good things happen, who is the first person you tell? When something goes wrong, who is the first person you call? Even though Jesus is God, although he was involved in orchestrating the plan of salvation, although he trusted God's sovereignty, although he knew his death would result in resurrection and eternal life – knowing all of this – when the hour came, he turned to his Father in prayer. He knew there was no-one better.

Yes, God knows your requests before you make them. Yes, he knows your thoughts even before you have them (Psalm 139:1–4). However, like a father, he delights to hear your voice; he wants to share intimate fellowship with you.

Speak to God throughout the day. When you receive good news, when you face a difficult task or when you are feeling lonely, turn to God first. Before you rush to other people for advice and affirmation, seek God. Let your prayer life prove to God that you know there is no-one better to trust with your joys and sorrows.

Day 26

Read John 17:1–26
Key verses: John 17:1–5

....

¹*After Jesus said this, he looked towards heaven and prayed:*

> *'Father, the hour has come. Glorify your Son, that your Son may glorify you. ²For you granted him authority over all people that he might give eternal life to all those you have given him. ³Now this is eternal life: that they know you, the only true God, and Jesus Christ, whom you have sent. ⁴I have brought you glory on earth by finishing the work you gave me to do. ⁵And now, Father, glorify me in your presence with the glory I had with you before the world began.'*

Is Jesus' passion for his own glory selfish and egotistical?

In this prayer, Jesus' first request is for his own glory. The Old Testament says that God does not share his glory with another, but Jesus unashamedly asks to be glorified. His two reasons are significant. He wants to be glorified so that the Father will be glorified (verse 1), and to bring people eternal life (verse 2). He wants God to be honoured and people to receive eternal life through his death and resurrection (verse 5).

Could Jesus really be glorified as he hung on the cross in excruciating pain and indignity? Yes! What bursts out of the cross is: this God must be loving and just. There's no sweeping of sin under the carpet. It is being graphically dealt with. And this God must be wise, because he is doing what nobody in the world can do, that is, to bring a perfect God and sinful people together. And this God must be powerful: millions and millions of people are going to live for eternity because this event has taken place at Calvary.

The prayer that Jesus would be glorified in his death was wonderfully answered. The cross screams the glory of God: his love, wisdom, power and justice. And when it is explained, the power of the gospel changes the way people think, understand and, God willing, live.

Jesus seeking his own glory wasn't egotistical. In fact, it was the exact opposite. It was a demonstration of his love for us. As John Piper explains,

God's passion for his glory is the essence of his love to us . . . God's love for us is *not* mainly his making much of us, but his giving us the ability to enjoy making much of him forever. In other words, God's love for us keeps God at the center . . . O how we need to help people see that Christ, not comfort, is their all-satisfying and everlasting treasure . . . Magnifying the supremacy of God in all things, and being willing to suffer patiently to help see and savor this supremacy is the essence of love. It's the essence of God's love. And it's the essence of your love. Because the supremacy of God's glory is the source and sum of all full and lasting joy.

(John Piper, 'How Is God's Passion for His Own Glory Not Selfishness?', www.desiringgod.org/articles/how-is-gods-passion-for-his-own-glory-not-selfishness, 24 November 2007)

Turn your eyes to the cross. See the lengths Christ went to so that you could savour the glory of God. And like Jesus on the cross, Paul's thorn in the flesh, Lazarus's death and countless other examples, God can and will use suffering to glorify his name. So don't long for comfort, security and a pain-free life. Choose to see even your troubles as opportunities to magnify God's name.

Day 27

Read John 17:6–19

Key verses: John 17:11, 15

....

> [11] *I will remain in the world no longer, but they are still in the world, and I am coming to you. Holy Father, protect them by the power of your name, the name you gave me, so that they may be one as we are one . . .*
>
> [15] *My prayer is not that you take them out of the world but that you protect them from the evil one.*

How do you usually pray for your children, parents, close friends and other family members?

Jesus had two prayer requests for his apostles. The first was that they would be kept or protected.

Jesus is not praying that the disciples will be kept from trouble; he knows most of them would be martyred. Rather, he wants them to be kept from the world (verse 11) and the devil (verse 15). 'Whatever happens to their bodies,' Jesus might be saying, 'guard their souls.'

And in verse 11, Jesus prays specifically that the Father will keep them 'by the power of your name', which, of course, means his character. Jesus is praying that the Father would keep the apostles by his faithful character, and God answered that prayer. All the evidence we have is that the eleven apostles were kept until the end.

I think this is a rebuke to our trivial prayers and the way we pray for our loved ones. When we live in reasonably good circumstances, we can easily absorb all the middle-class bourgeois trivia of the world around us. And we find ourselves praying that our children would be happy and successful, although we don't put it quite as boldly as that. Our prayers are not much different from what pagans would want for their children. Do you see the sting of this? Do you want your children just to be happy and successful? What about wanting your child to be kept so that even if he or she is martyred before they reach thirty-five years old, God is glorified. That's a brave prayer; that's a Bible prayer.

As we have seen, God's glory does not come cheaply. It usually involves pain, suffering and sacrifice. Knowing the full impact of this, it is one thing to pray that *our* lives would glorify God; it is quite another to pray that God would be glorified in the lives of *those we love*. Allow the Holy Spirit to challenge how you pray for your loved ones:

> Perhaps we should pray harder prayers for our children. Perhaps we should pray for the kind of ride which will bring them greatness of character. Perhaps we should pray that their self-confidence is dented so that they learn to lean on God more and find in him their strength and their portion, even if that means that some of their hopes and dreams, and ours, have to come crashing down.
>
> (Ann Benton, *Parenting against the Tide*, Evangelical Press, 2014).

Today, choose one of the apostle Paul's prayers and look at what he asks God for (see Ephesians 1:15–21; 3:14–21; Philippians 1:9–11; Colossians 1:9–12). If it is helpful, use his prayer as a model, praying what he prayed for your loved ones.

Day 28

Read John 17:6–19
Key verses: John 17:17, 19

· ·

[17] Sanctify them by the truth; your word is truth . . .
[19] For them I sanctify myself, that they too may be
truly sanctified.

Not many of us would describe ourselves as 'prayer warriors'. In fact, we may feel our prayer life is pretty inadequate. But don't lose heart!

Jesus' prayer for his disciples was very simple. It contained only two requests: first that they would be 'kept', and second that they would be 'sanctified'.

What does it mean to be sanctified? God sanctifies in two ways. One way is to get into position, to be set apart for Jesus (1 Corinthians 6:11). It's like picking a special team: 'We're going to set a group apart for this particular job. We're going to devote them to this task.' The other way God sanctifies is to make people holy by a process:

it's the process of being transformed into the likeness of Christ (1 Thessalonians 5:23). Position or process – now which is it here?

I think he wants them to be in position, because in verse 19 he says, 'I sanctify myself.' Jesus does not need to make progress in his character. He doesn't need to improve in his likeness of God; he's positioning himself. He has set himself apart to do God's will. He is saying, 'I put myself in position so that they may be sanctified. I am going to go where I should be, the cross, so that they will be where they can be, which is in your family.'

In order to stay in this position, the apostles need 'the truth' (verse 17). This is the truth that Jesus has been talking about in John 14:15–16: the Spirit will enable the apostles to record the truth, the words of Jesus, the life of Jesus, and this will result in the Old and New Testaments. This truth will keep them for the task, so that they know who they are, why they are there, what they are doing, why they are doing it and where it will all end.

We too need to learn the truth if we are going to do our task in the world.

: Jesus' followers will be 'set apart' from the world,
: reserved for God's service, insofar as they think and
: live in conformity with the truth, the 'word' of revelation

(verse 6) supremely mediated through Christ (himself the truth, 14:6, and the Word incarnate, 1:1, 4) – the revelation now embodied in the pages of this book.
(Don Carson, *The Gospel According to John*, IVP, 1991, p. 566)

So what better prayer could we pray for our loved ones than Jesus' own simple prayer: 'Keep them, sanctify them'?

As our prayer goes up, the Father graciously hears us, and the thousand darts being aimed at that man or woman are diverted. The temptation that is going to face them down the street finds no great interest in them. The sinful impulse that we all look for a way to indulge gets no opportunity. The things of Jesus suddenly appear very wonderful, and the things of this world look very small and temporary because the Father has heard someone pray, 'Keep them, sanctify them.'

Start a habit today. Each time you pray for your loved ones, ask God to 'keep them and sanctify them'.

Day 29

Read John 17:20–26
Key verses: John 17:20–23

....

> ²⁰ *'My prayer is not for them alone. I pray also for those who will believe in me through their message,* ²¹ *that all of them may be one, Father, just as you are in me and I am in you. May they also be in us so that the world may believe that you have sent me.* ²² *I have given them the glory that you gave me, that they may be one as we are one –* ²³ *I in them and you in me – so that they may be brought to complete unity. Then the world will know that you sent me and have loved them even as you have loved me.*

Jesus knows us well.

He knows all our flaws – our desire for recognition, our tendency to want our own way, our slowness to say 'sorry'.

Not surprisingly, then, Jesus' prayer for believers down through the centuries, including us, starts with a request for unity – 'that all of them may be one' (verse 21).

Importantly, our unity is to be grounded in the truth (verse 20). We need to belong to the same apostolic message. That's why we need to keep humbly reading our Bibles. God has made us one family by his Spirit. We may disagree on lots of things, but we are still family. The only way to stay united in heart and mind is by sitting under the Bible and reading it humbly together. The Word of God is going to make us not just family, but a mature family. We are not just going to be united in the Spirit; we are going to be united in the truth. Jesus explains that unity is possible because he's given us the truth (verse 22). He says, 'I've given them the revelation of myself: I've shown them what I think, what I say and what I do. I've given them the glory, the revelation.'

But this unity is not just in the truth; it is relational, as Jesus explains in verse 21: 'Father, just as you are in me and I am in you. May they also be in us.' The bonds we have with other believers might be very superficial. But in a thousand years we'll enjoy fellowship which will be so close, so special, so rich, so perfect that we won't believe it. That's what God has begun: relational unity. And this unity is also progressive. In verse 23, Jesus prays, 'May they be brought to complete unity.' This is not just spiritual unity, but being one in heart and mind as the Scriptures are heeded.

'Wounded by friendly fire' could describe many of us in the church. We have been hurt by the comments and behaviour of other believers, and it is hard to keep working towards unity. But don't give up! Unity is our witness to the world. It is deeper than differences over worship styles and any number of other secondary issues that cause controversy. As Paul reminded the Galatians, our unity is based on Christ (Galatians 3:28–29).

Meditate on Philippians 2:1–5 and ask God how you can contribute to unity in your church:

> Therefore if you have any encouragement from being united with Christ, if any comfort from his love, if any common sharing in the Spirit, if any tenderness and compassion, then make my joy complete by being like-minded, having the same love, being one in spirit and of one mind. Do nothing out of selfish ambition or vain conceit. Rather, in humility value others above your-selves, not looking to your own interests but each of you to the interests of the others.
>
> In your relationships with one another, have the same mindset as Christ Jesus.

Day 30

Read John 17:20–26
Key verses: John 17:24–26

· ·

24 Father, I want those you have given me to be with me where I am, and to see my glory, the glory you have given me because you loved me before the creation of the world.

25 Righteous Father, though the world does not know you, I know you, and they know that you have sent me. 26 I have made you known to them, and will continue to make you known in order that the love you have for me may be in them and that I myself may be in them.

At the age of eighty-one, when the well-known preacher Martyn Lloyd-Jones was at the end of his life, his friends and family gathered round him. Many people thought they should be praying for a miracle. But apparently Lloyd-Jones wrote a shaky little note to his wife telling them not to bother because he didn't want to be kept from glory!

Arriving in glory was Jesus' prayer for each one of us (verse 24). Why are we going to arrive? Because Jesus went through the crucifixion: 'I go to prepare a place.' He did it; he prepared a place. He didn't prepare a place for good people or successful people. He prepared a place for believers.

Do you wonder sometimes whether you will ever be in glory? Do you wonder sometimes whether there is a glory? Jesus prays for us to be taken to glory, and every single prayer he has prayed has been answered. He prayed for himself to be glorified on the cross: he was. He prayed to be glorified back with the Father: he was. He prayed for the apostles to be kept: they were. He prayed for the apostles to be sanctified: they were.

Notice verse 24: Jesus doesn't say, 'Father, I'm asking.' Do you notice the words? He says, 'Father, I want', and the phrase in the original is: 'I will it.' Jesus says to the Father, 'I'm telling you what my will is. I will that they be with me.'

One day we will arrive in heaven. Until then, run your race well!

: Jesus' death on the cross and his prayers for you are
: your guarantee of glory. One day you will arrive in
: heaven. That's the end of the story, but what happens

in the meantime? Well, Jesus is at the Father's side interceding for you. His work of sanctification is on-going. As Paul said, 'He who began a good work in you will carry it on to completion until the day of Christ Jesus' (Philippians 1:6). What is our role? Are we just to wait passively with our eyes on the horizon? No! Because we are bound for heaven, Peter urges us, 'You ought to live holy and godly lives as you look forward to the day of God and speed its coming' (2 Peter 3:11–12). Whatever today holds for you, ask God to help you to keep your final destination in mind.

For further study

If you would like to do further study on John's Gospel, the following may be useful:

- Don Carson, *The Gospel According to John* (IVP, 1991).

- Kent Hughes, *John: That You May Believe*, Preaching the Word (Crossway, 2014).

- Colin Kruse, *John*, Tyndale New Testament Commentaries (IVP, 2008).

- Bruce Milne, *The Message of John: Here Is Your King*, The Bible Speaks Today (IVP, 1993).

KESWICK MINISTRIES

Our purpose

Keswick Ministries is committed to the spiritual renewal of God's people for his mission in the world.

God's purpose is to bring his blessing to all the nations of the world. That promise of blessing, which touches every aspect of human life, is ultimately fulfilled through the life, death, resurrection, ascension and future return of Christ. All of the people of God are called to participate in his missionary purposes, wherever he may place them. The central vision of *Keswick Ministries* is to see the people of God equipped, encouraged and refreshed to fulfil that calling, directed and guided by God's Word in the power of his Spirit, for the glory of his Son.

Our priorities

Keswick Ministries seeks to serve the local church through:

• *Hearing God's Word*: the Scriptures are the foundation for the church's life, growth and mission, and *Keswick Ministries* is committed to preach and teach God's Word in a way that is faithful to Scripture and relevant to Christians of all ages and backgrounds.

- *Becoming like God's Son*: from its earliest days the Keswick movement has encouraged Christians to live godly lives in the power of the Spirit, to grow in Christ-likeness and to live under his lordship in every area of life. This is God's will for his people in every culture and generation.

- *Serving God's mission*: the authentic response to God's Word is obedience to his mission, and the inevitable result of Christlikeness is sacrificial service. *Keswick Ministries* seeks to encourage committed discipleship in family life, work and society, and energetic engagement in the cause of world mission.

Our ministry

- *Keswick: the event.* Every summer the town of Keswick hosts a three-week Convention, which attracts some 15,000 Christians from the UK and around the world. The event provides Bible teaching for all ages, vibrant worship, a sense of unity across generations and denominations, and an inspirational call to serve Christ in the world. It caters for children of all ages and has a strong youth and young adult programme. And it all takes place in the beautiful Lake District – a perfect setting for rest, recreation and refreshment.

- *Keswick: the movement.* For 140 years the work of Keswick has impacted churches worldwide, and today the movement is underway throughout the UK, as well as in many parts of Europe, Asia, North America, Australia, Africa and the Caribbean. *Keswick Ministries* is committed to strengthen the network in the UK and beyond, through prayer, news, pioneering and cooperative activity.

- *Keswick resources.* *Keswick Ministries* produces a range of books and booklets based on the core foundations of Christian life and mission. It makes Bible teaching available through free access to mp3 downloads, and the sale of DVDs and CDs. It broadcasts online through Clayton TV and annual BBC Radio 4 services.

- *Keswick teaching and training.* In addition to the summer Convention, Keswick Ministries is developing teaching and training events that will happen at other times of the year and in other places.

Our unity

The Keswick movement worldwide has adopted a key Pauline statement to describe its gospel inclusivity: 'for you are all one in Christ Jesus' (Galatians 3:28). *Keswick Ministries* works with evangelicals from a wide variety of church backgrounds, on the understanding that they share a commitment to the essential truths of the Christian faith as set out in our statement of belief.

Our contact details
T: 01768 780075
E: info@keswickministries.org
W: www.keswickministries.org
Mail: Keswick Ministries, Convention Centre, Skiddaw Street, Keswick CA12 4BY, England

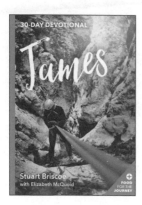

related titles from IVP

FROM THE FOOD FOR THE JOURNEY SERIES

James
Stuart Briscoe
with Elizabeth McQuoid

ISBN: 978–1–78359–523–5
112 pages, paperback

The Food for the Journey series offers daily devotionals from much-loved Bible teachers at the Keswick Convention in an ideal pocket format – to accompany you wherever you go.

'I was truly encouraged as I used this each day, and discovered fresh insights into the letter from James.' Peter Maiden, International Director Emeritus, Operation Mobilisation, and Minister-at-Large, Keswick Ministries

'"Faith in working clothes" is an apt description of this letter of James. This helpful, practical guide will encourage you to get your hands dirty for the Lord while keeping your heart clean. Warmly recommended!' Dr Steve Brady, Principal, Moorlands College, Christchurch

Also available

2 Timothy
Michael Baughen with Elizabeth McQuoid
1 Thessalonians
Alec Motyer with Elizabeth McQuoid
John 14 – 17
Simon Manchester with Elizabeth McQuoid

Related Teaching CD Packs

James

Stuart Briscoe
SWP2239D (4-CD Pack)

John 14 – 17

Simon Manchester
SWP2238D (5-CD Pack)
SWP2238A (5-DVD Pack)

Also available

2 Timothy
Michael Baughen
(SWP2202D 4-CD Pack)

1 Thessalonians
Alec Motyer
(SWP2203D 5-CD Pack)

Available from www.essentialchristian.com

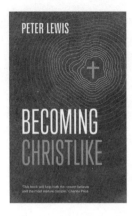

related titles from IVP

KESWICK STUDY GUIDE

Transformed

Becoming like God's Son

Derek Tidball

ISBN: 978–1–78359–454–2

80 pages, paperback

Becoming like Jesus requires us not just to meet him occasionally but also steadily and surely to 'remain' in him.

How does this look close up?

In a world where Christlikeness is counter-cultural, the author offers sure-footed Bible teaching, questions, illustrations, suggestions and prayers to point us in the right direction. And, as well as this useful material, we have the Holy Spirit's help to live transformed lives today.

This practical, thought-provoking and accessible resource is the latest in the popular IVP/Keswick Ministries series of study guides.

'Yes, the terrain is challenging. But this is a grace-filled, Christ-dependent journey to become more like Jesus. Come join!' Tracy Cotterell